A CAT'S LIFE

Using this book

To make this book a truly
personal record of your cat, put
your own photographs in the paw prints
or 'picture frames', writing in captions on
the toe prints or around the photograph,
and jot in your own notes where suggested.
Use a piece of tracing paper to mark the
size of the paw prints so that you can use it
as a template when cutting out your
photograph. A cat has nine lives, so
celebrate each one of them!

To Clement, Maeve and Mahni, three exceptionally cool cats

Ailsa Greenhalgh

A CAT'S LIFE Celebrate the life of your pet

with illustrations by Rowan Barnes-Murphy

Quadrille

'Cat: a pygmy lion who loves mice, hates dogs, and patronises human beings.'

Oliver Herford (1863-1935)

Contents

This book is dedicated to the life and times of

place a photo here

'All animals are equal but some animals are more equal than others.' George Orwell (1903-1950) *Animal Farm*

Address: Distinguishing features

Breed: Birthday:

Part 1
Me, Myself and I

My unique personality

'The smallest feline is a masterpiece.'

Leonardo da Vinci (1452-1519)

My pleasures in life:

The imperfections in my day:

Why I am adored:

Pursuits I will never tire of:

My most glorious moment (according to me):

Kitty pic'n'paw

'If a dog jumps in your lap, it is because he is fond of you;
but if a cat does the same thing, it is because your lap is warmer.'

Alfred North Whitehead (1861-1947)

place a
paw print here

Height:

Weight:

Favourite hiding place:

Purring moments:

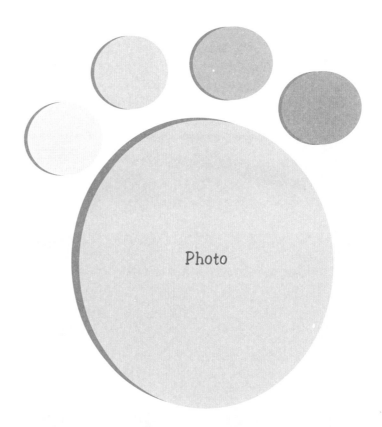

Photo

'I cannot agree that it should be the declared public policy of Illinois that a cat visiting a neighbour's yard or crossing the highway is a public nuisance. It is in the nature of cats to do a certain amount of unescorted roaming ... to escort a cat abroad on a leash is against the nature of the owner. Moreover, cats perform useful service, particularly in the rural areas. The problem of cat versus bird is as old as time. If we attempt to resolve it by legislation who knows but what we may be called upon to take sides as well in the age old problems of dog versus cat, bird versus bird or even bird versus worm. In my opinion, the State of Illinois and its local governing bodies already have enough to do without trying to control feline delinquency.'

Adlai Ewing Stevenson (1900-1965) As governor of Illinois, vetoing a bird-protection bill

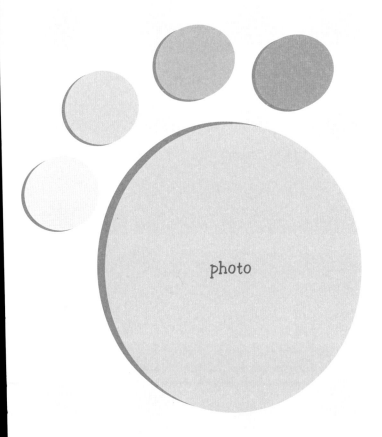

Filthy furball

'But I was thinking of a plan, To dye one's whiskers green.'

Lewis Carroll (1832-1898)

photo

Spaces I like to fill with mucky paw prints:

Places I like to malt most:

photo

My close shaves

(a page to record my nine lives)

'The cat has nine lives: three for playing, three for straying, three for staying.' English Proverb

Puffed and fluffed

'He that lies down with dogs, shall rise up with fleas.'

Benjamin Franklin (1706-1790)

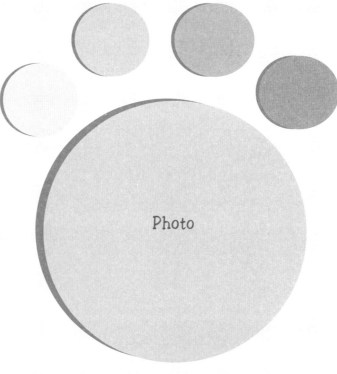

Photo

Photo

Pampering techniques that win me over:

My attitude towards hygiene:

Gribouille - the well-travelled cat

Gribouille was only a kitten when his elderly owner Madame Martinet gave him away. Although he went to live with her next-door neighbour, a local policeman, the wall between their houses would not keep Gribouille from his old home. He would often visit his mother and be found lying in his favourite resting place, on the thyme plants at the base of the plum tree in Madame Martinet's garden.

A few weeks later his new owner was transferred from Tannay, in Central France, to Reutlingen, a town in the South West of Germany, and Gribouille was forced to leave behind his stomping ground. Madame Martinet thought the move had gone well until she received a letter from the policeman saying that Gribouille had gone missing three weeks after their arrival.

For one year and nine months Gribouille was not seen or heard of, until an extremely malnourished cat, with sore feet and infected eyes, turned up on Madame Martinet's doorstep. She didn't recognise the cat in front of her but Gribouille's mother rushed up straight away and began to lick him, knowing that it was her son who had come home. Gribouille headed to the thyme plants to lie down and Madame Martinet realised her old kitten had made a remarkable journey to be with them.

In fact Gribouille had travelled over 1,000 kilometres in two years, crossing major roads, rivers and international borders. Even though he travelled to Germany in a car, he managed to find his way across this huge distance and then succeeded in pinpointing the exact location of his home.

Gribouille was nursed back to health and Madame Martinet let him stay in one place for the rest of his days.

Part 2
Feline Folk

Members of my family

'I love cats, because I love my home,
and after a while they become its visible soul.'

Jean Cocteau (1889-1963)

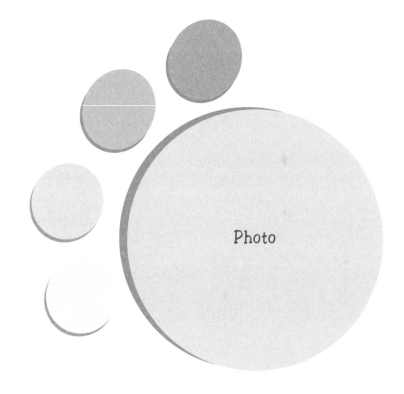

Photo

Photo

Photo

Photo

'A house without a cat, and a well-fed, well-petted, and properly
revered cat, may be a perfect house, perhaps, but how can it prove its title?'

Mark Twain (1835-1910) *The Tragedy of Pudd'nhead Wilson*

My family tree

Draw in my family tree, getting in as many of my aunts,
uncles, brothers, sisters and grandparents as you can.

'The gentlemen will please remember that when his half-civilised ancestors were
hunting the wild boar of Silesia, mine were Princes of the earth.'

Judah P. Benjamin (1811-1884)

Photo

My animal ancestors

'God has created the cat to give man the pleasure of caressing the tiger.'

Theophile Gautier (1811-1872)

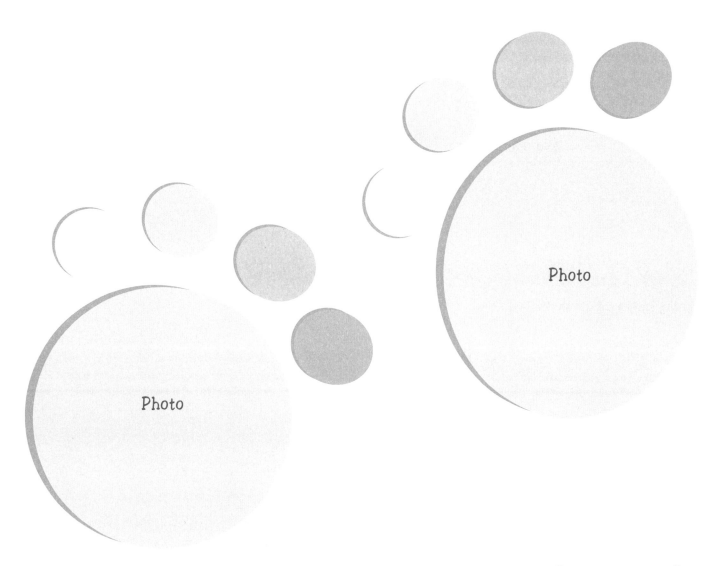

Photo

Photo

My four-legged friends

`When the cat and mouse agree, the grocer is ruined.`

Iranian Proverb

`Cat-speak`

(write in the way I communicate these phrases to my humans)

`Did you say treat?`

`Let's play.`

`I'd like some love and attention`

MIAOW!

`That's my lounging area`

`I'm embarrassed but I'm pretending I'm not`

`Don't even think I'm interested`

Parent pic'n'paw

'The cat is the only non-gregarious domestic animal.
It is retained by its extraordinary adhesion to the comforts
of the house in which it was reared.'

Francis Galton (1822-1911) *Inquiries Into Human Faculty*

place a
Paw print here

Height:

Weight:

Occasions I like to employ selective hearing:

Furniture I like to damage:

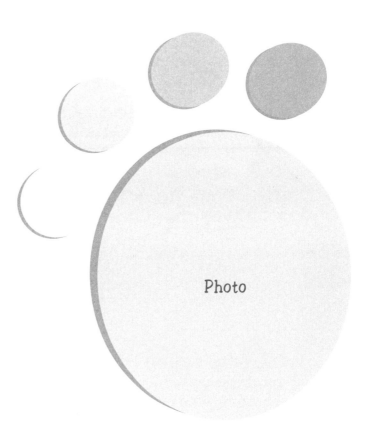

Photo

"All right" said the [Cheshire] cat; and this time it vanished quite slowly,
beginning with the tail and ending with the grin, which remained some time after the rest of it had gone.'

Lewis Carroll (1832-1898) *Alice in Wonderland*

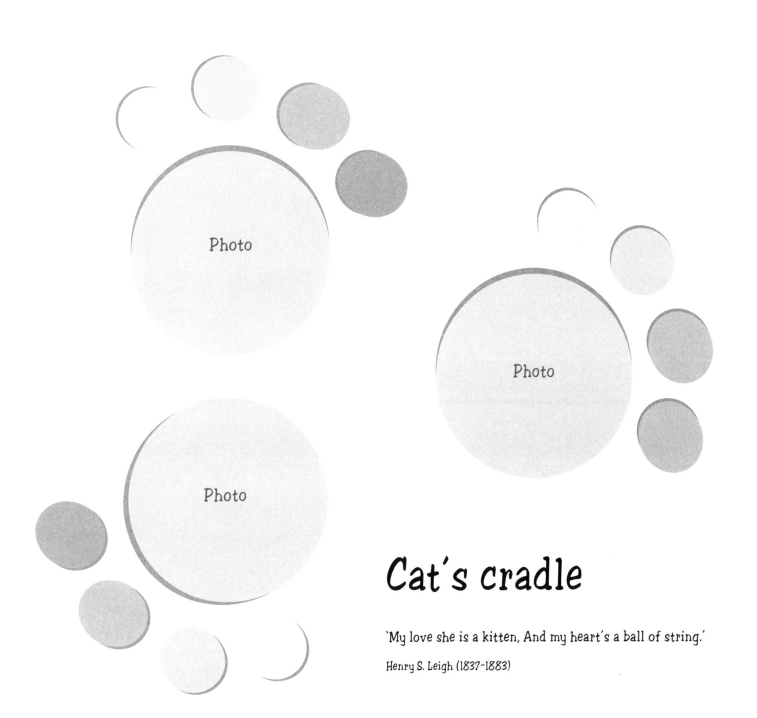

Photo

Photo

Photo

Cat's cradle

'My love she is a kitten, And my heart's a ball of string.'

Henry S. Leigh (1837-1883)

The legend of the beckoning cat

The temple of Gotoku-ji in the Japanese province of Setagaya was very poor and the monks had little or no food, but despite the desperate situation the master priest shared his food with his pet cat. One day this cat was sitting in the doorway of the temple and a group of Samurai rode up. The cat had its paw raised up to its face, as though it were greeting them and beckoning them in. The group took it as a sign of invitation and stopped at the temple to rest. In doing so they avoided the lightning of an unexpected storm and the torrential rain forced them to stay. While they were there the priest gave them tea and taught them something of the Buddhist philosophy.

After this, one of the Samurai, Lord Li, regularly returned to learn more about Buddhism from the master priest and eventually endowed the temple with a large estate and made it the property of the Li family. In fact the family were buried there and near their tombs a small shrine was built to the memory of the Beckoning Cat.

The image of the cat with its paw raised is called the Maneki Neko. It is considered to be a lucky charm for the Japanese, firstly because the cat saved the Samurai's lives by beckoning them in from the lightning of the storm, and secondly because the cat brought prosperity to the poor temple and harmony into the life of Lord Li.

Today the Gotoku-ji Temple still stands in what are now the suburbs of western Tokyo. The exterior of the temple is festooned with pictures of the Maneki Neko and the interior is filled with statues of the beckoning cat and prayer boards from owners who want to pray for their own cats.

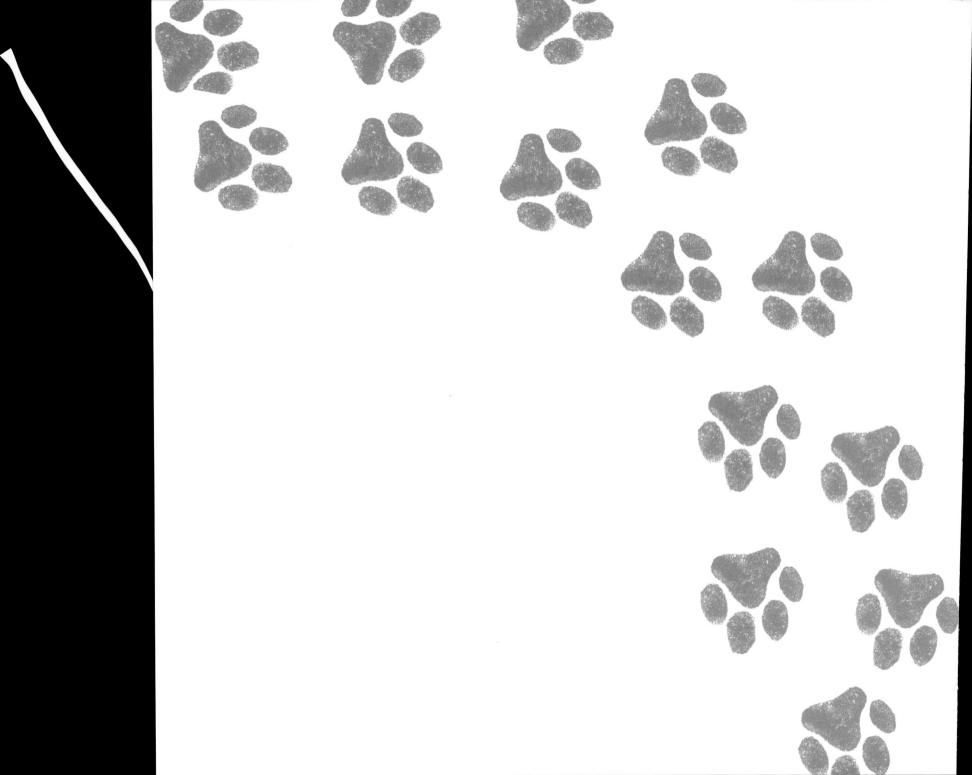

Part 3
Pussycat Pastimes

Wherever I lay my hat

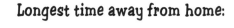

Longest time away from home:

Favourite cattery:

My travelling essentials:

'I travel not to go anywhere, but to go. I travel for travel's sake. The great affair is to move.'

Robert Louis Stevenson (1850-1894) *Travels with a Donkey*

The Owl and the Pussy-Cat

'The Owl and the Pussy-cat went to sea
In a beautiful pea-green boat,
They took some honey, and plenty of money,
Wrapped up in a five-pound note.
The Owl looked up to the stars above,
And sang to a small guitar,
'O lovely Pussy! O Pussy, my love,
What a beautiful pussy you are,
You are,
You are!
What a beautiful Pussy you are!'

Pussy said to the Owl, 'You elegant fowl!
How charmingly sweet you sing!
O let us be married! too long we have tarried:
But what shall we do for a ring?'
They sailed away, for a year and a day,
To the land where the Bong-tree grows
And there in the wood a Piggy-wig stood
With a ring at the end of his nose,
His nose,
His nose,
With a ring at the end of his nose.

"Dear Pig, are you willing to sell for one shilling
Your ring?" Said the Piggy, 'I will.'
So they took it away, and were married next day
By the Turkey who lives on the hill.
They dined on mince, and slices of quince,
Which they ate with a runcible spoon;
And hand in hand, on the edge of the sand,
They danced by the light of the moon,
The moon,
The moon,
They danced by the light of the moon.'

Edward Lear (1812-1888)
   The Owl and the Pussy-Cat

Photo

Feline fancies

Pussy Potage
(Serves one)

Ingredients
2 tinned sardines
2oz butter
1 cup water
a sprinkling of baby spinach leaves

Method
Place the sardines and butter into a frying-pan on a medium heat. Mash the sardines in with the butter as it melts, making a pulp. When the butter has melted entirely, pour in the water and stir as you bring the broth to the boil. Throw in the baby spinach leaves. Take the pan off the heat and allow the mixture to cool. Liquidise the broth until smooth and serve at room temperature.

'The cat loves fish, but hates wet feet.' Italian Proverb

Nice Mice Bites

(Serves one)

Ingredients

1 egg
2 tablespoons oatmeal
3oz sausage meat / mince beef
sprinkling of catnip, finely chopped
(optional)

Method

Mix the ingredients together well in a bowl. Take teaspoons of the mixture, one at a time and knead into tiny mice shapes. Grill under a medium heat for 5-7 minutes, turning them regularly, until the outsides are crisp. Allow them to cool. If the mice bites are still too big for your cat to eat, then slice them into more manageable chunks.

Food I'll never touch in a month of Sundays:

Feline fancies I'm prepared to be loving for:

'Kissing don't last; cookery do!' *George Meredith (1828-1909) The Ordeal of Richard Feverel*

My entertainment

'When I play with my cat, who knows whether
I do not make her more sport than she makes me?'

Michel Eyquem, signeur de Montaigne (1533-1592)
Book ii. Chap. xii. Apology for Raimond Sebond.

Games I relish:

My favourite hunting targets:

Toys I can get my claws into:

Sleeping hours

'It is no small art to sleep: to achieve it one must keep awake all day.'

Friedrich Nietzshe (1844-1900) *Thus Spake Zarathustra*

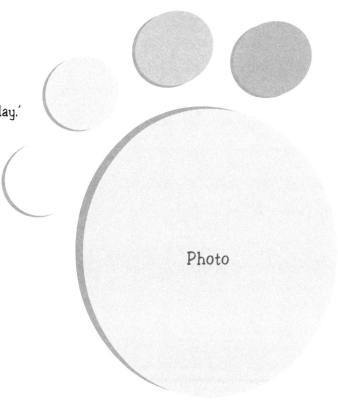

Photo

Photo

My favoured sleeping positions:

My designated lounging areas:

Soft spots

(a page to record my favourite tickling and scratching areas)

'After all perhaps we have no greater enjoyments among us than those of eating when we are hungry.
...lying down when sleepy, or as the second Solomon has pronounced than scratching where it itches.'

Abraham Tucker (1705-1774) *The light of nature pursued*

Senior pic'n'paw

'I don't generally feel anything till noon, then it's time for my nap.'

Bob Hope (b.1903)

place a
paw print here

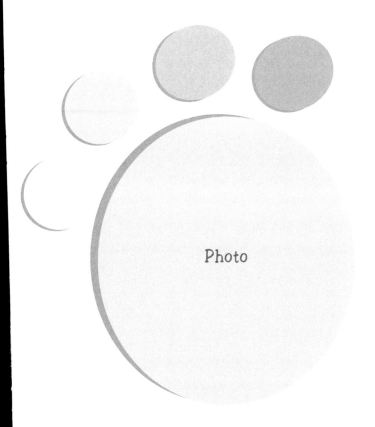

Photo

Height:

Weight:

Important daily and nightly rituals:

Average napping hours per day:

Faith – the cat with a holy hunch

Faith was a pretty tabby-and-white stray who adopted Reverend H. Ross, the rector of St. Augustine's Church in the City of London, and who became a heroine after her intuition saved both her own and her kitten's life.

Faith lived with the Reverend in his rooms at the top of the Church House and would often wander into the church to sit in a pew and listen to the choir or the services. In the summer of 1940 she gave birth to a tiny black-and-white kitten called Panda. But on Friday, September 6th, Faith became restless and frantically searched all the corners of the house. Eventually she lifted her kitten out of its basket, carried it down three floors, and placed it in an alcove in the wall where the rector stored his sheet music. Reverend Ross took the kitten back up stairs four times, but Faith kept returning the kitten to the alcove until the Reverend gave in. He had the hiding place cleared and put the cat's basket there instead.

Three nights later, in a heavy bombing raid, the Church Rectory was hit exactly where Faith's basket had originally been. The house caught fire immediately and when the rector returned the next day burning rubble was all that was left. The firemen were convinced that Faith and her kitten would not have survived the blast, but when they left Reverend Ross climbed on the rubble to check for himself. He called Faith's name and heard a faint 'miaow' in return. Miraculously, the alcove had not collapsed and he saw Faith under all the smouldering debris sitting serenely, protecting Panda between her paws, as she had undoubtedly done all night. It seemed that Faith's 'premonition' and her ability to find a safe hiding place had saved her own life and that of her kitten.

After Faith's ordeal the PDSA awarded her a silver medal to commemorate her bravery. It was engraved with the words 'For steadfast courage in the Battle of London, September 9th, 1940' and it hung in the chapel of the church, alongside Faith's picture, until the church was eventually demolished.

'Der spring is sprung,
Der grass is riz,
I wonder where dem boidies is?

Der little boids is on der wing,
Ain't dat absoid,
Der little wings is on der boid!'

Anonymous.

Cat contacts

Vet/practice: **Tel:**   Sitter:

Illnesses / inoculations / operations

Visit date   Treatment   Beauty Parlour:

                                                              Holiday Home:

                                                              Friends:

                                                              Neighbours:

Pet Charities and Organisations

UK

Association of British Veterinary Acupuncture
tel: 020 7937 8215

Association of Pet Behaviour Counsellors
tel: 01386 751151
web: apbc.org.uk

Association of Private Pet Cemeteries
tel: 01342 712976

Blue Cross Animal Hospitals
tel: 020 7834 4224
web: thebluecross.org.uk

Cat Action Trust
(re-homing/neutering feral cats)
web: cat77.org.uk

Cat Protection League
tel: 01403 221900

Cat Welfare Trust
tel: 01278 427575

K9to5 (London pet-care agency
for your pet's daily needs)
tel: 020 7368 6622
email: k9tofive@hotmail.com

Department for Environment, Food and
Rural Affairs (DEFRA)
(contact for information about pet travel)
tel: 0870 241 1710
web: defra.gov.uk

Pet Bereavement Support Service
tel: 0800 096 6606

People's Dispensary for Sick Animals
(for owners unable to afford vet bills)
tel: 0800 731 2502
web: pdsa.org.uk

Pet Education
(information on all aspects of pet care)
web: peteducation.com

Pet Health Council
tel: 01476 861379
web: pethealthcouncil.co.uk

Royal College of Veterinary Surgeons
(vet information)
tel: 020 7222 2001
web: vetweb.co.uk

RSPCA (inquiries)
tel: 0870 444 3127
web: rspca.com

Australia & New Zealand

Animal Rescue Inc.
(shelter for pets and native
animals in New Zealand)
tel: 03 6368 1310

Australian Animal Protection
Society
tel: 03 9798 8415
web: aaps.org.au

Australian Cat Federation Inc.
tel: 08 8449 5880
web: acf.asn.au

Australian Veterinary Assoc.
tel: 02 9411 2733
web: ava.com.au

Feline Information
(offers advice on the care of
cats and kittens and conducts
ongoing reviews of laws
relating to pets)
tel: 03 6239 1666

Government information
web: pets.info.vic.gov.au

Humane Society International
(animal welfare)
web: hsi.org.au

Humane Society of NZ Inc.
(fosters and re-houses dogs and
cats, and runs a telephone
advisory service)
tel: 09 630 0510

The Lonely Miaow Association Inc.
(pet rescue, adoption and shelters
in New Zealand)
tel: 09 575 9760

National Pet Loss Grief Hotline
(open from 8-10pm Sydney time)
tel: 02 9746 1911

Pet Education
(information on all aspects of pet care)
web: peteducation.com

PetNet
(everything about caring for your
pet in Australia and New Zealand,
with links to other sites and
useful organisations)
web: pet-net.net/australia

Pets at Peace
(specialist pet cremations)
tel: 1800 63 6797

RNZSPCA (Inc.)
(umbrella body in New Zealand for
50 local and city Societies for the
Prevention of Cruelty to Animals)
tel: 09 827 6094

RSPCA
tel: 02 6282 8300
web: rspca.org.au

Second Chance Pet Sanctuary
(rehoming)
tel: 07 5522 9720
web: scps.bizland.com

South Africa

Animal Behaviour Consultants
of South Africa (ABC)
web: animal-behaviour.org.za

International Fund for Animal Welfare
(IFAW offers advice for animal care in
numerous countries, including South Africa)
web: ifaw.org

Johannesburg SPCA
(offers a lost-and-found service,
shelter and adoption)
tel: 011 681 3600
web: jspca.org.za
email: jspc@icon.co.za

Pet Education
(information on all aspects of pet care)
web: peteducation.com

PetNet
(everything about caring for your pet
in South Africa, with links to other
sites and useful organisations)
web: pet-net.net/south_africa

First published in 2001 by Quadrille Publishing Ltd

Alhambra House

27-31 Charing Cross Road

London WC2H 0LS

ISBN 1 903845 09 2

Printed and bound by Monheim GmbH in Germany

Many thanks to Jessica at Scrivo and to all those who gave permission for the quotes included within
this book: p6, *Animal Farm* by George Orwell (Copyright © George Orwell 1945) reproduced in the UK and
Europe by permission of A M Heath & Co. Ltd on behalf of Bill Hamilton as the Literary Executor of the
Estate of the Late Sonia Brownell Orwell and Martin Secker & Warburg Ltd, and reproduced in the United
States by permission of Harcourt, Inc.; p11, Alfred North Whitehead, from *Dialogues of Alfred North
Whitehead* published by Little, Brown & Co. Ltd; p20, Jean Cocteau, by permission of Eric Glass Ltd; p41,
Bob Hope, by permission of the International Herald Tribune.